A Century of Premiers

Also by Dick Leonard

THE BACKBENCHER AND PARLIAMENT (ed. with Val Herman)
CROSLAND AND NEW LABOUR (ed.)
THE ECONOMIST GUIDE TO THE EUROPEAN UNION
ELECTIONS IN BRITAIN: A Voter's Guide (with Roger Mortimore)
GUIDE TO THE GENERAL ELECTION
PAYING FOR PARTY POLITICS
THE PRO-EUROPEAN READER (ed. with Mark Leonard)
THE SOCIALIST AGENDA: Crosland's Legacy (ed. with David Lipsey)
WORLD ATLAS OF ELECTIONS (with Richard Natkiel)